Practical UX Bits for Novices and Experts

101 Random UX Tips

By William Ntim

101 Random UX Tips - By William Ntim

Copyright ©2020, by William Ntim. 101 Random UX Tips - Practical bits for novices and experts.
All Rights Reserved. No part of this publication may be reproduced, stored in retrieval system, or transmitted in any form or by any means; electronic, mechanical, photocopying, recording, or otherwise; without prior written permission.
First Edition

Printed in the United States of America
Cover Design: Eden Ntim

*Dedicated to my wife, Eden.
Thank you for your support and this amazing book cover.*

Also, to every Software Designer out there, I hope this book provides you with useful insights and tips to make you more efficient and proficient.

Table of Contents

Tip 1 - Your Approach 13
Tip 2 - Push-backs 14
Tip 3 - Past Life 15
Tip 4 - Aesthetics 16
Tip 5 - Ultimate Tip 17
Tip 6 - Stakeholders 18
Tip 7 - Research 19
Tip 8 - Observation 20
Tip 9 - Competitive Analysis 21
Tip 10 - Ego 22
Tip 11 - Users 23
Tip 12 - Error Messaging 24
Tip 13 - Punctuation 25
Tip 14 - Portfolio 26
Tip 15 - Design Process 27
Tip 16 - Balance 28
Tip 17 - Users 29
Tip 18 - User Testing 30
Tip 19 - Collaboration 31
Tip 20 - Consistency 32
Tip 21 - Cognitive Bias 33
Tip 22 - Design Hygiene 34
Tip 23 - Suggestive Dropdowns 35
Tip 24 - Trends 36
Tip 25 - Minimalism 37
Tip 26 - Job Application 38
Tip 27 - Bootcamp 39
Tip 28 - Recruiters 40
Tip 29 - Curiosity 41
Tip 30 - Portfolio 42

Tip 31 - Cust. Journey 43
Tip 32 - Order/Sequence 44
Tip 33 - Post Deployment 45
Tip 34 - Data-Driven 46
Tip 35 - To Reinvent 47
Tip 36 - Color/Vision 48
Tip 37 - Display Hierarchy 49
Tip 38 - Scrolling 50
Tip 39 - New Tools 51
Tip 40 - Reading 52
Tip 41 - Shadows 53
Tip 42 - White Space 54
Tip 43 - Accessibility 55
Tip 44 - Tools vs Skill 56
Tip 45 - Ultimate Tool 57
Tip 46 - Human-Centeredness 58
Tip 47 - Size Hierarchy 59
Tip 48 - User Activity 60
Tip 49 - Mobile 61
Tip 50 - Confirmation 62
Tip 51 - Consistency 63
Tip 52 - Call-to-actions 64
Tip 53 - Responsiveness 65
Tip 54 - Micro-interactions 66
Tip 55 - Lorem Ipsum 67
Tip 56 - Opt-in 68
Tip 57 - Reinvention 69
Tip 58 - Conversion 70
Tip 59 - Problem Statement 71
Tip 60 - Call-to-actions 72

Table of Contents (cont'd)

Tip 61 - UX or UX 73	Tip 83 - Leaving a company 95
Tip 62 - E-Commerce 74	Tip 84 - Device Mock-ups 96
Tip 63 - Directions/Tool-tips 75	Tip 85 - Portfolio Role 97
Tip 64 - Learning Curve 76	Tip 86 - Tools 98
Tip 65 - Display Architecture 77	Tip 87 - Community 99
Tip 66 - System Status 78	Tip 88 - User Testing 100
Tip 67 - Mobile 79	Tip 89 - UX World 101
Tip 68 - Sticky Magic 80	Tip 90 - Assessment 102
Tip 69 - Breadcrumbs 81	Tip 91 - Job Search 103
Tip 70 - Contract/Full-time 82	Tip 92 - Portfolio 104
Tip 71 - Mobile Hover 83	Tip 93 - Why UX? 105
Tip 72 - Mobile Modal 84	Tip 94 - Metrics 106
Tip 73 - User Attention 85	Tip 95 - Int. Prototypes 107
Tip 74 - Interaction Time 86	Tip 96 - Productivity 108
Tip 75 - Documentation 87	Tip 97 - Interviews 109
Tip 76 - Execution 88	Tip 98 - Interviewing 110
Tip 77 - Dev Teams 89	Tip 99 - Company Sizes 111
Tip 78 - Work Attachment 90	Tip 100 - Create Content 112
Tip 79 - Listen Actively 91	Tip 101 - Stakeholders 113
Tip 80 - Portfolio 92	
Tip 81 - Mental Health 93	
Tip 82 - Job Search 94	

Tip 1 - Your Approach

The way you approach a problem is a major part of your role as a UX Designer. This thought process and approach shapes the direction of your output and results. Being an Experience Designer means you create for users regardless of industry, topic, or platform, and therefore, a 'one-size-fits-all' mentality might do some projects injustice.

Every industry is different and so is every product and platform. Your ultimate skill is your critical thinking approach to each problem statement. This will guide you to the right process and execution toward desired objectives.

Use this time to read more, broaden your knowledge-base and expand your technical skills beyond visual design. It exposes you to a better understanding of our world and human behavior which comes into play when designing for Human-Computer interaction.

Think clearly and rationally about each problem statement. Approach it from a place of ignorance but with intent to fully understand all aspects of the problem and the solution needed.

Remember, no two projects are the same.

Tip 2 - Push backs

Know when to give in to push backs. Not everything is black and white from the exterior. A UX superpower is learning to understand valid technical or organizational obstacles that could hinder or delay your desired solutions to go to market as soon as you wish.

Before a product or feature can successfully go to launch, several factors come into play, such as budget constraints, technical constraints, market shifts, stakeholder diversions, leadership change, user-behavior changes, and many more. It sure is a draining feeling knowing all the hard work you put into a project was in vain. I've been there, and it's very unpleasant.

Nonetheless, it is important to face the music and embrace this reality that sometimes, products or features fail to ship, and that's okay. More often than not, these blockers are beyond our control, especially when leaders allow their egos and preferences to dictate feature releases hence the necessity to be mentally prepared for when it happens.

The end goal is not to give in and be a pushover but to harness the power of knowing when to let go, wait, or press on.

Change takes time, sometimes.

Tip 3 - Past Life

Do not deny your past. If you have experience in other fields, embrace it, and identify how these experiences or skills can be useful in your UX career. Highlight them in your portfolio and share insights into tips or lessons you've learned along the way.

Be cautious though, to keep in mind that not everything is UX. Mislabeling certain experiences could skew the message you're trying to send and reflect badly on your expertise.

It is important to respect the sovereignty of each industry, even when identifying similarities. Human behavior is a constant, regardless of industry, and provides a wealth of knowledge to benefit from.

Ultimately, this past life is YOUR experience, and being able to articulate how it has influenced your work puts you in a good light and makes you stand out.

There's only one of you, so let us know the real you behind the UX.

We're waiting.

Tip 4 - Aesthetics

The aesthetics of your UI matters — a lot.
Humans are visual creatures, and creating for Human-Computer Interaction means taking into account your design solutions' aesthetics. Having impeccable design skills and a strong eye for beautiful, sharp and accessible interfaces will set you apart from the rest.
Use this time to practice and refine your visual design skills.

Apart from conducting peer design challenges, there are lots of online resources that provide great design practice avenues such as:
- Uplab
- DailyDesign Challenges
- CollectUI
- Adobe Daily Design Challenge
- 100 Days of Product Design

The last tip to improve design skills is studying Style Guides. Download guides from major companies and study how they build each component, the thought behind each element and how these elements come together to compose the pleasant experiences we use daily.

Do beautiful work; it's a reflection of you.

Tip 5 - Ultimate Tip

As User Experience professionals, our titles usually define our priority --when the hiring team does their job, of course. Many designers ask what the ultimate tip is, and the simple answer is there is none. I say this because every UX tip will always have "supporting tips" to go along with it for successful execution. It's like cooking a meal; some chefs may say the sauce is the ultimate ingredient, but there are always other ingredients in every good meal.

Nonetheless, there is an underlying tip that I believe all designers can cultivate, and that is putting the user first. It's a very simple statement but one that comes with a not-so-simple execution process. Ensuring that we put our users first is our topmost priority. Unless in scenarios where our titles require otherwise.

A Product Designer will most likely put the product and stakeholder needs first, whereas a User Experience Designer is hired to put the user's needs first. Know who you are designing for and put them first. Are you designing for a new product and therefore prioritizing stakeholder goals or vice versa?

How you put the user first is another story. There are several tips in this book and other books that will help you achieve this. The crux of this tip is to:

Know who you're designing for, and put them first.

Tip 6 - Stakeholders

Defending your UX solutions at your workplace requires storytelling. Knowing who your audience is internally and how to deliver your case is critical to creating change for better UX.

Designing beautiful or effective experiences is one thing, but selling that to your stakeholders is another. As designers, we sometimes forget that we can treat our stakeholders as "users" and approach our final presentations/meetings like we would any other UX project.

Dive into your stakeholder's needs and find out what matters most to them in the entire project. Extract ways by which you can align your project delivery to speak to their individual expectations and values. This places your best foot forward and the stakeholder in question may be more keen to lean in and consider your design solutions.

By the way, this is not a magic trick. The tip here is to dig deeper into our stakeholders' values and speak to them in a manner that elevates the design decision we are presenting.

Not everyone is out to get you; sometimes, empathizing with the stakeholder/decision-maker in your pushback makes all the difference in getting the buy-in you're looking for.

Tip 7 - Research

Research never ends. It is not a one-and-done activity. It is a revolving cycle that must continue even after deployment or launch. For the optimum user experience and to keep the user centered throughout your product's life — at all times, put measures in place to gather feedback and research on your users' behavior.

We see this done a lot in recent days, where websites will integrate third-party survey tools within the e-commerce journey to collect usability data during checkout. This type of research is most likely conversion-based. There are other scenarios where companies would further ask a customer for product feedback after purchase right after asking them how smooth their browsing experience was.

You could say too much research doesn't hurt, as long as the user has the option to opt-out. The upside of having measures in place to collect behavioral data is that your design decisions become closely accurate in satisfying your users' needs.

Don't stop observing, talking, and listening to your users. This is how you build an incredible product that will churn the returns you desire while benefiting your users at the same time.

Refer to Page 18 for supporting tip.

Tip 8 - Observation

Observing your users produces the best research results. Even better, observing them incognito generates the purest, most authentic form of feedback one can obtain. Hence helping you pinpoint the actual problem your customers are facing. Of course the method by which this is done needs to take into consideration user privacy, respect, and legal limitations.

I prefer this method than asking users for feedback directly through surveys or moderated sessions because they put users under some or a lot of pressure when done poorly. Their responses can also be skewed based on the setting or compensation involved. In-browser session recording tools are wonderful examples of tools that provide authentic user reactions and feedback by just watching and studying the user as they navigate through your product.

Even in field research, if you can set it up so that you're not hovering over the user with a camera, laptop and tablet but rather allowing them to operate as they would naturally, you would garner some pretty authentic and raw results.

Remember, Science is defined as a study of the physical and natural world through observation and experiment.

Observation is pure.

Tip 9 - Competitive Analysis

Please do not perform Competitive Analysis before you start sketching, ideating, or concepting. This practice is flawed and will hurt your ability to avoid any cognitive bias during the creation process. A lot of designers are quick to check what competitors are doing as soon as they are presented with a problem-statement. That's quite an unhealthy approach. This causes bad UX on a large scale because ineffective UX gets duplicated until it becomes accepted as the norm.

When you are presented with a problem statement, gather all the research you can and obtain a thorough understanding of your users' problem. Then proceed to sketch, ideate and concept solutions based on that data. After you have explored a few options, you can then perform Competitive Analysis to either validate or take away from what you have already designed based on effectiveness and research.

It is difficult and impossible to avoid Cognitive Bias completely, but it is important to reduce the prominence of it in restricting your originality and creativity.

You are a UX pro because of your skill and ability to create. Put that to work first before opening the door to external influences or what's being done elsewhere.

This is an effective way to innovate and lead.

Tip 10 - Ego

Your ego as a Senior UX professional is detrimental to effective UX. Though vital and priceless, our wealth of experiences can interfere with actual user needs in situations where we place our preferences before research data. Even when the data contradicts with best practices and outcomes we've known to be true for years.

I doubt this is something we purposefully do - myself included. Somehow ego finds a way to creep in and get in the way of seeing things clearly in a new project. Consistent success can be blinding to new terrain. This tip is only a reminder to regain awareness and allow the data/user to drive our design operations and decisions even in situations we've been in over and over again.

There is beauty in your ability to go wherever the data leads. Especially if this means ruling out your own proposed design solutions for something better, it is not weakness, but rather strength.

User behavior can be very volatile, staying current on behavioral data to inform design solutions instead of ego and "status-quo" will do you a lot of good in the long run.

Be data-informed, always.

Refer to Page 17 for supporting tip.

Tip 11 - Users

Users don't always like change. If it's not broken, don't fix it. Humans are creatures of habit. Unless your major or minor feature change is an absolute necessity that will improve user satisfaction, it is better to abandon, postpone, or release these updates in substantial phases. A seemingly tiny change like a hue update can make or break an experience for your users.

Ensuring that feature updates are absolute necessities require validation from user data. Follow the lead of the users as they guide you to weak and ineffective features in your software experience.

On the other hand, if you're going to change a feature or part of an experience, make that change worth it - like night and day. Test this change and refine it to suit desired user success.

Do not be afraid to create change — but rather, do it with caution. As always, allow the data to guide you.

When in doubt, data.

Refer to Page 18 for supporting tip.

Tip 12 - Error Messaging

Do not overthink your error messaging. Keep it simple, direct, obvious, and language accessible. You'll see a spike in improved user experience if you prioritize user comprehension of your error messages.

You can achieve this by being direct when communicating an error to your user. Direct in the form of error language, placement, and accessibility. Ensure that the message is easy to understand, and that the user knows exactly the location of the error in the experience and how to resolve it.

For instance,
> "*Your password is invalid. Passwords must contain two numbers, one uppercase, and one lowercase character. Please check and retry.*"

...will be easily understood to the average user rather than,

> "*Error 00f2x3483xyz! Password is invalid.*"

Please note though, that depending on who your end-user is, "*Error 00f2x3483xyz! Password is invalid.*" might be a better fit if the application is meant for developers, etc. who understand what that means.

Identify your user and prioritize their comprehension.

Tip 13 - Punctuality

Punctuality is a vital soft skill for every UX professional. Time is valuable. Your product team may be lenient but are you honoring your agreement with the team on time?

Attendance, meetings, design deliverables, interviews, are all time-sensitive, and respecting the value of such time is a priceless asset for any UX professional.

The future started yesterday, don't be late.

Tip 14 - Portfolio

Your Food Delivery, Dating App, Music Player Concept Design looks pretty nice but so does that of several other portfolios out there. This is not a knock on designers who have such samples in their portfolio but rather a nudge to venture out into uncommon grounds.

Maybe some Finance Management interfaces, Education Technology, Auto Dealership portals, Ballot Management interfaces, unique Ticket Management for events, Credit Score Management UI's, Government tools, Real Estate interfaces etc.

You could even take this a step further by redesigning some interfaces recognizable by your ideal company/industry to work for. Unless your perfect industry includes the ones I mentioned previously, feel free to venture outside the box. After all, the goal is to set yourself apart.

Go, create, and explore.
Your portfolio is a safe space.

Tip 15 - Design Process

Your UX design process is not a ritual.
The usual Empathize, Define, Research, Wire-frame, Lo-fi, Hi-fi etc. sure are proven steps that generate the best outcomes but your thorough understanding of the relevance of each step is the key to amazing experiences.

The UX career journey will throw odd scenarios your way that will require you to either alter, skip, rearrange or abandon certain steps entirely. Some companies may require you to perform these steps at a faster pace than usual, while others may grant you all the time in the world to dig deeper into every step of the design process.

Your ability to discern when to refine your process without sacrificing quality will affect your efficiency and value in the industry.

Know when, to do what and how.

Tip 16 - Balance

Great experiences are usually the most well-balanced. Without a strong core foundation, your design will be easily swayed in every direction like a feather in a windstorm. In other words, combining too many ingredients can cause your meal to taste awful.

Too much simplicity or minimalism, and you risk retaining the user's attention. Too much complexity and you risk ease-of-use. Too much color, contrast, saturation, or lack thereof and you risk accessibility. Too futuristic, and you may be doing too much.

Whether Libra or not, remember to balance the design scale. Observe the flow of your breath, become aware of your power to add and subtract.

Namaste.

Tip 17 - Users

Some users do know exactly what they want. Creating design solutions that satisfy "our" perception of a user's needs defeats the entire purpose of "user-centered" design. We hear this statement a lot that customers don't know what they want but based on who the customer is, they sometimes do know exactly what they want.

Listening to the user and empathizing involves being able to decipher when to give the customer what they ask for and when to build solutions around the ask.

The issue with basing design decisions solely on user requests or survey data is that sometimes, the ask doesn't fully represent what the user's core need is. Employing a variety of research and testing efforts will help clarify and validate proposed user needs.

Being the experience professional, a key part of your role is your ability to decipher when to give the customer what they ask for and when to build solutions around the ask.

Either way, know your customer.
There is never a one-size-fits-all.

Refer to Page 18 for supporting tip.

Tip 18 - User Testing

Avoid being hasty to user testing. There are key steps that need to be taken during the design process before testing can be effective. Rushing through the process could skew your solutions, testing and results.

User Testing is a very important part of our process to validate proposed solutions. How these tests are crafted, and what they consist of, are all factors that need to be well-refined before launching a user test.

Some designers advocate for testing even when an interface is incomplete. Others advocate for rapid testing - a concept that certainly speeds up the process but may omit critical checkpoints. As long as designers ensure that the initial steps of defining the problem, identifying the user, scoping out the project, identifying the market and competition, sketching, flow charting, etc are all executed effectively, then rapid testing will be a great addition to completing the final prototypes.

I'm not a huge fan of following too many rules, but when it comes to the UX design process, certain boxes have to be checked to ensure effective outcomes.

Before you test, exhaust the rest.

Refer to Page 25 for supporting tip.

Tip 19 - Collaboration

Invite collaboration. Even if it's only a "critique" session, you will receive invaluable feedback that could point out relevant gaps or add improvements to your solution.

You don't have to implement every suggestion, but receiving feedback could even trigger other ideas you may have missed. In cases where you can, the diverge and converge method could also serve you well in acquiring a variety of solution ideas from your team.

Every member of your product or broader team has a unique thought-process, experience, and perspective on the product, user, and life in general. I cannot stress enough how valuable this can be to the success of your experience design.

It is okay to let others in on what you're building. Be proud to share the progress. Welcome collaboration and feedback.

You still remain the final decision-maker in adapting any feedback or ignoring them. In the end, two heads are better than one.

Tip 20 - Consistency

Consistency in brand UX design is vital but not at the expense of effective UX. When gaps within an experience are ignored for the sake of consistency, you run the risk of a catastrophe waiting to happen. On the other hand, brand integrity can be lost when interface experiences are inconsistent. Color, Typography, Illustrations, Alignment, Element and Layout Design are all components that contribute to a consistent experience throughout an application.

This is also an area of balance. Necessary problem-areas/elements can be updated and released in parts while respecting brand guidelines closely as possible. Sometimes, an update to certain components entirely may be needed.

The value of this change must outweigh the value of keeping the interface brand-consistent. If prioritizing consistency will translate better in improving your users' experience, then that must take priority over introducing new element/interface design treatments.

Your end-goal is for your experience to be a success, so monitor that goal closely and how it meets your users needs.

Keyword: "YOUR".

Tip 21 - Cognitive Bias

Here's how I reduce cognitive bias when creating design solutions. Firstly, I harvest the fruits of my mind, keep them in a safe place, and then continue to reap the fruits of other amazing minds via collaboration, competitive analysis etc.

I harvest my mind by creating wire-flows and sketches of design concepts in isolation and storing them on whiteboards, sketchpads, paper, etc. You can still do this at work, just find an empty room where you won't be disturbed, or simply put on some headphones. This is only to keep you focused and uninterrupted while you ideate, brainstorm, and sketch.

The next step will be to open up the space and invite team collaboration, Competitive Analysis or any other external influences.

This, I have found to be effective in somewhat reducing biases in my creative thinking. The irony of this tip is the assumption of having no or less bias, which in turn validates blind spot bias.

Oh well, what can I say?

Tip 22 - Design Hygiene

Practice good design hygiene. This is a loose term representing the conscious effort of a designer to organize, label, store properly and secure their design files before, after, and during the design process.

Here's what I mean; before you begin designing, ensure that the file you're creating is labeled correctly and saved in the right folder, which is also labeled correctly, and saved in a properly labeled parent-folder as well. Labeling correctly is subjective to what you would understand but a good rule of thumb is to label your file with recognizable breadcrumbs such as Current Date, Project Name, Project Version, Company Name etc. The way by which you combine these breadcrumbs is up to you.

Certain designers will do Project Name and Project Version in the sub-folder, and do a Company Name, Current Date in a parent-folder.

For instance, great design hygiene will exhibit itself in the labeling and storing of a file in the following path:

WilliamCorp-->2020-->WebFiles-->HomepageRedesign_v1

A poorly organized, labelled and stored file system will make a designer's job harder later on when unexpected updates arise. It also makes it more difficult for other team members to pick up from where someone left off.

Organization is key.

Tip 23 - Suggestive Dropdowns

The fact that drop-downs get their own tip reveals how big of an issue this can be. Suggestive Drop-downs have come to help users but have also failed in accounting for other "use-cases". If you're not familiar with suggestive drop-downs, these are drop-downs that allow you to enter two or three characters before auto-loading with suggested results.

You enter the letters "W, i, l," in such a field and it returns drop-down results like "William, Wilson, Wilfred, Willow," etc. An amazing feature, but is it better than a regular, traditional drop-down? It depends, I'll say.

When designing for suggestive drop-downs, please ensure that the drop-down also has a scroll bar that allows the user to scroll through all the results prior to entering any characters.

The second part is to ensure that the results are in alphabetical order regardless of quantity. Some users may not know the correct spelling of what they are searching for (humans can be forgetful) hence granting them the ability to scroll through the results as they would in a traditional drop-down can be very helpful. You could also add some image references to the results if the data allows it. It helps make results easily identifiable and beautiful at the same time.

Lastly, account for technical failure where data fails to load based on character entries. What happens then? Can the user save their entry and proceed or do they have to select the next close option? Lot's to think about for suggestive drop-downs.

Tip 24 - Trends

As the saying goes, there is nothing new under the sun. Many design trends and "UX trends" have come and gone. Some stayed longer than expected, and others lasted long enough to be featured in a couple of articles.

It may be a hot UX trend, but that does not mean it is good for your users. "Good" as in effective, appropriate, and beneficial.

Some trends evoke so much excitement and promise but like everything else, be sure to vet and validate UX trends with your users before making a grave mistake.

Nonetheless, stay trendy.
Just as long as it aligns with your user needs.

Tip 25 - Minimalism

"Minimalism" in UX design is vital but not at the expense of effective UX. When gaps within an experience are ignored for the sake of minimalism, you run the risk of a catastrophe waiting to happen. On the other hand, overcrowding an interface could lead to a catastrophe as well.

Once again, find the balance. Essential components that are highly necessary for task completion should take priority. Everything else can follow accordingly. If the interface begins to get crowded, the least components that directly affect task completion should be cut.

Avoid being so minimal that the user has to overthink about proceeding to the next step of your interface journey. I've seen experiences that try to "hide" too many elements in favor of keeping things "clean" but end up with miserable users who have no idea where anything is.

In the end, your Return On Investment for effective UX will justify sacrificing some "cool" elements.

Tip 26 - Job Application

Job searching is a daunting experience. We have all been there; both senior and junior designers go through difficult times when job searching. Some are worst than others but strategic perseverance is what separates the successful applicants from the rest.

I will address a few tips on this subject but the first one is to apply for jobs you are qualified for. Many designers fail to assess their true level of expertise and apply for jobs outside their current skill level. The reality is you probably will not qualify for every role with "UX" in its title. This applies to junior designers as much as it applies to senior designers.

Take the time to read through each job description, making a note of all requirements and keywords. Compare this with your original resume, skill-level, and be honest with yourself if this is a role you will excel at. It is important to honestly answer this question because to pretend to be skilled at something in order to get the job is a dangerous game. You don't want to end-up not living up to the expectations set for the role.

Aside from saving time for the right jobs, this process will also help you identify gaps in your skill-set that need filling. Focus on what you are good at, and pursue roles that align with your current skill-set.

Refer to Page 92 for supporting tip.

Tip 27 - Bootcamp Experience

Deciding to continue education in any field is a powerful step toward success. I am very proud of all Bootcamp graduates that have gone through the mental prep and physical prep of immersion into the great world of UX.

One thing that I have noticed on resumes or social profiles of Bootcamp graduates that I think may be sending the wrong message is adding your Bootcamp education tenure as an "experience". A few graduates that I have spoken to say that bootcamps actually asked them to go ahead and enter it this way.

Here is my take on that, education is education, and hence the categorization of education and experience being in different sections on a resume or profile. The message this sends to me is a designer trying so hard to justify their education experience as a professional experience in order to get the job. Most hiring managers like myself, find this a little inaccurate. Imagine a law school student entering their years of education at Law School as "experience". It does not send the right message and it does not belong there.

Be proud of your Bootcamp education and categorize it as education because professional experience is far different than education experience. If you are lacking in having any professional experience, there are other ways to fill this void.

Refer to Page 105 for supporting tip.

Tip 28 - Recruiters

Recruiters do not owe you anything during a job search. I see many viral posts bashing recruiters on how one response was too vague or another was incomplete.

Job searching can be a pain, and it's easy to find someone to blame, but the reality is that a recruiter has one job and that is to find the perfect candidate for a role.

Even if they receive a thousand perfectly qualified candidates, they still have a responsibility to choose only one. You are either the one chosen or one of the rejected.
It's a hard reality but also the difficulty of their job.

I understand the frustration of not knowing exactly why an application was rejected; on the other hand, recruiters receive hundreds and sometimes thousands of applications to review. To expect detailed responses for every single one is nearly impossible if we're honest.

Let us be more human to recruiters because as of now, most of them are human too.

Tip 29 - Curiosity

    Be curious about everything. When we were kids, we were fascinated by the things around us, how the world worked and even how humans functioned. Interestingly, our curiosity seems to decline as we get older. We become more set in ways, perspectives and ideals than we were younger.

    This tip is a reminder to reignite that curiosity. The inquisitiveness that drives you to want to find out more about something strange, new, bold or daring. Whatever comes your way as you go through this life, open yourself to learning more about it even if it's for understanding how things work or the perspective of others.

    This knowledge, especially about people and things, comes in handy in the weirdest times during your User Experience career as you build amazing things using technology for humans. A crazy fun app that you discovered months ago could be the trigger that spurs a new feature in your experience or a different perspective on technology from someone could spark a new idea for your next project.

    Everything around you has something to offer.
Be curious, cat - you're safe here.

Tip 30 - Portfolio

First impressions are everything. This applies to the digital world, as well. Your portfolio is the next opportunity you have to connect with a recruiter after they receive your application and resume. This is your opportunity to make a mark. Make sure your portfolio has a wow-factor!

This tip will be a little difficult to explain since the wow-factor of two different portfolios can be two completely different things. The mission here is to ensure that when a hiring manager first lands on your portfolio homepage, they are "wowed" upon their arrival. Something unique, something that is memorable, and something that is you.

I've seen designers do this by adding a fun gif of themselves in their "element.": which could be the outdoors, dance, biking etc. Others also use animated components to add a moment of delight to the homepage. You could also add a wow-factor through the text or language used on the page. Current affairs are also a great pool of content to choose from. The possibilities are endless, and this is also an opportunity to get creative.

Don't overthink it, but think about it.
How do you want to stand out?

Tip 31 - Customer Journey

We like to design amazing customer journeys but sometimes we forget that the customer may not always follow our application experience journey like we intend them to. This is a reminder to design for the "What-if's".

This is not a list to check off but some examples to get you thinking through various scenarios of the customer experience that could be contrary to the road we expect the customer to travel.

Here are some examples:
- What if the user decides to click outside of the box?
- What if they decide to abandon the application entirely and return to the previous screen?
- What if the user wants more information but would still like to continue from where they stopped afterwards?
- What if the user landed in or exited the experience by mistake?
- What if the user would like to finish later?
- What if the server fails to return the data requested?
- What if the user waits too long before taking the next action?
- What if?

Tip 32 - Order/Sequence

The order of executing UX methodologies can affect bias which in turn affects the output. There is a reason why our industry has accepted certain key steps as a golden rule to get us to the expected outcomes. For instance, accurately defining the problem-statement is a critical piece to designing the right solutions. That's why it must be performed as the first step.

Creating hi-fi comps is usually saved until the latter part of the process because it is very time-consuming and relies heavily on approved wire-frames. Information Architecture, user testing, customer journeys, user personas etc. Doing this very early on could be a waste of time and resources.

Conducting research to help define the problem-statement and also identify customer personas are always better performed prior to any design work.

There are circumstances though that may require the designer to skip or alter certain steps and that's understood, but the overall sequence must still be preserved in its right order for the best outcomes.

Study the sequences of the best processes out there and dig deeper into why one is better performed before the other. There is magic in the sequence.

Refer to Page 25 for supporting tip.

Tip 33 - Post Deployment

One major mistake most designers make is failing to follow up on projects after shipping or deployment. A designer's work is not done even after the product has shipped. Regardless of the presence of a QA team, it is in our best interest to check in and review the finished experience.

Between hi-fi comps and development, things do get lost in translation. Your pretty work may not be coded exactly as you designed it. The layout and alignment may be off, so could the padding, margins, shadows, etc. Reviewing the live experience unearths any errors that arose during development.

We love developers, but our keen eye for design is something we mostly possess. On the other hand, when you find any issues with the developed experience, remember to address those gently and precisely so that your developers can accurately make the required changes.

This is a normal part of the process. Nothing to be alarmed about if things don't look exactly like you expected it to. It may also require aligning design and development tools so closely as to avoid this happening again in future.

Be a team player but keep an eye on your baby even as it goes into the wild.

Tip 34 - Data-Driven vs Data-Informed

Use a data-informed approach rather than being solely data-driven. Though making design decisions based on data is the appropriate method of creating amazing experiences, how this data is harvested plays an integral role in the success of the experience. Let the data inform your decisions and not solely drive them.

There's not a huge difference between the two but being data driven means we deliver exactly what the data says - as long as the data says "X" we deliver "X". On the other hand, being data-informed means we could implore a variety of options that would satisfy the problem and even solve for other hidden problems at the same time based on what the data shows.

We take what the data shows us, and synthesize it by digging deeper into validating what we think the data is trying to tell us, compare that against any errors or bias that could have influenced the data, apply our expertise and understanding of human behavior and, finally, create a solution that aligns perfectly with the problem.

Next time you obtain data, dig deeper, extract understanding that aligns with your user needs, validate your synthesis, infuse your expertise and best practices, test your solutions, and deliver a fitting experience that goes above and beyond your user's expectations.

Tip 35 - To reinvent or not to reinvent

Do not limit yourself to standard UI components, styles and features. Free yourself to explore and create outside of the widely used interface standards. Engagement and great experience are what we design for but innovation will take us to the next stage of human-computer interaction.

There are reasons why the majority of set standards work, but they can also be a stepping stone to a great redesign. Of course, the timing of such "reinvention" is critical to your experience so avoid confusing your users with new ideas that haven't been tested, tried and proven. Your reinventions can also be tested and validated before launching them throughout an application.

I challenge you to question everything, and explore other ways by which a user's life can be made even easier during human computer interaction. This could unlock so many ideas that might benefit us all.

You are a creator; do not be afraid to create.

Tip 36 - Color and Vision

Not every human has regular vision; ensure that your interface will be visible and legible for all vision types - Design for color-blind users. A great rule of thumb is to not only use color as the differentiator of important elements but to add an extra modifier like an icon or underline.

There are a few different types of color blindness types, namely Deuteranopia, Protanopia, Tritanopia and Monochromacy. Each type renders the individual unable to experience the entire color spectrum in its fullness and beauty.

Fortunately for all, various modern tools now make it easy to test for vision compatibility within our prototypes during the design process. This is one important step to making your experiences accessible because not all humans enjoy the same level of senses. The extra time you spend on fine-tuning your experience for accessibility, makes a user's life easier, which was your goal in the first place.

Another quick trick to test for color visibility is to convert your entire design to gray-scale and verify if all elements are still visible. You could also create alternate color versions or "dark themes" if you have the time and resources.

Always design with all user groups in mind.

Tip 37 - Display Hierarchy

Consider the one-at-a-time rule. Displaying components in order of priority, whether it means showing them one at a time, using layers, or depth of field; the user's experience is streamlined and task completion becomes a lot easier.

Studies have shown that giving the user too many options affects the rate of task completion, conversion and the speed of completion. Users may back out of an experience if they have to think too much to continue to the next step.

Scenarios where display hierarchy has been applied effectively can be seen in pop-up modals where the background is blurred or opacity is reduced. Other examples include online forms that only display one form-field at a time which must be completed before the next field is displayed. The list goes on and on. Focus on what the priority hierarchy is at each experience level and explore ways by which you could enhance important tasks, elements, etc.

The human attention span is reducing daily; focusing on what's absolutely necessary at each level can be helpful.

Tip 38 - Scrolling

Use double scrolling carefully. It is very difficult to navigate, especially on mobile. Designers are leaning more towards alternatives to double-scrolling between the varying sizes of fingers and the unreliability of computer mouse and touch pads.

The overflow of information and legal requirements that govern our digital experiences today leaves us with no choice but to get creative when presenting large volumes of information. Having a scroll bar within a sub-section of a parent section which also has a scroll bar presents a major navigation challenge - one as difficult as this feature is to explain.

Understandably, there are times when the double-scroll feature is the only option available due to different constraints, but if this feature is going to be used, please ensure that users can clearly distinguish between the parent and child scroll bars. In some situations, a modal popup, new or collapsible section is a better solution.

Conduct some moderated or recorded user tests to verify usability with your users.

Tip 39 - New Tools

Learn new tools. This makes you more marketable and also secures your career. Tools are not the determining factor of your success in UX but your versatility will go a long way.

Aside from learning new tools for the benefit of being versatile, you also reap the benefit of being up-to-speed on new technological advancements. Many new tools boast of upgraded features and functions that become useful in creating experiences as time goes by.

The other factor is that UX roles also morph along with new technological updates - something the majority of companies will begin hiring for. You definitely want to strategically position yourself for when this occurs.

To everything there are pros and cons but the foundation of this tip is to prioritize your skill so that regardless of the tool you find yourself using, you can still deliver incredible work that generates effective results.

Please understand that by no means am I suggesting you must learn new tools to be successful. You can still be highly successful by specializing in one particular tool. Large, enterprise-level programs are slow to release updates anyway so specializing in one tool does have its benefits.

Study the market, and study your abilities. Understand that part of our success strategy may be to learn new tools.

Tip 40 - Reading

Prioritize reading - read more. Not only must you read more User Experience books but also psychology and books on human behavior. The word "read" here is used lightly. Immerse yourself into a deeper understanding of how humans, things and technology works.

As UX professionals, we build for humans, and that's why human psychology and computer interaction should be top of our list. In addition to that, I challenge you to read across other disciplines - ones that relate to our industry and others that don't. You will learn a thing or two which can be very beneficial in your design decisions.

Reading also keeps your brain active. It is essentially a workout for your brain. Similar to physical exercises, you keep your brain in shape when you engage in reading regularly. I used to hate to read. I hated writing; I hated organizing and everything in-between. Somehow, once you start reading more, you open yourself to thoughts and concepts that "jog" your cognition to go the extra mile during your brainstorming and ideation sessions.

You never know what you'll find or learn when you open a book.

Tip 41 - Shadows

Ensure that your shadows generally come from one source. Though shadows are a great addition to interface components, not using them correctly can damage the aesthetics of your interface.

There are exceptions if multiple light sources are used on purpose, of course. We live on a planet with one primary light source at a given time, and most humans use this concept of light and shadows to identify depth, position, dimension etc. visually.

This is a useful general tip but polishing certain shadows with multiple light sources to fit a specific look is also accepted. Use your design eye and decide accordingly.

Another important tip about using shadows is to avoid using them as the sole differentiator for important elements or call-to-actions. Design interfaces that are accessible.
Let shadows play a role but not the only role when it comes to telling things apart. Gray-scale is always your friend when in doubt.

> Whether one or fifty shades,
> use one general light source.

Tip 42 - Negative/White Space

Do not be afraid to use negative space positively. Additionally, do not forget to account for negative space in your designs. For those unfamiliar with the term, this is mostly the white space or blank areas seen throughout a layout or design piece.

It appears in various forms such as padding, margins, line-spacing, and element/component spacing. Designers use this to create breathable room around design elements. It makes it easy to read the text, navigate and even identify grouped elements.

The best example is the paragraph spacing throughout this book. We used indented paragraphs and one line spaces between each paragraph to make it easier to read. Every paragraph is also generally centered around one focal point which helps the reader group the ideas shared in each paragraph.

I urge you to dig deeper into negative spaces and how they can be used to convey a variety of messages, increase usability and even drive users to perform specific tasks in an experience.

In the meantime, give your design elements some breathing room. It surely is one of the secret sauces to good design.

Tip 43 - Accessibility

Make your designs accessible. Digital accessibility is simply designing for everyone. Humans are creatures of different abilities and disabilities. Designing for everyone means taking into consideration the effective usability of your experiences by all types of people including those with visual, hearing, speech, or cognitive impediments.

Thankfully, doing this is now easier than ever before during your design process. Always refer to the WCAG (Web Content Accessibility Guidelines) on w3.org to stay up-to-date on current accessibility tips and best practices. Below are some high-level methods by which you can make your experiences accessible as you create them:

- **Check the contrast ratio:** Ensure that your interface has enough distinguishable contrast between elements.
- **Always add alternative captions to your images.** This makes it easy for reading applications to read out the content of the image.
- **Label your form-fields using appropriate "label" tags.** Be cautious about using placeholders as labels. Reading apps are unable to identify these.
- **Hover and focus states:** Include focus states for all action elements and support keyboard navigation
- **Code markup:** Work with developers to make sure the content markup is accurate and comprehensible.
- **Apps:** Use modern tools to audit your design work for accessiblity before handing over to development.

Lastly, conduct accessibility research to get more data and understanding from your users to guide your design direction moving forward.

Tip 44 - Tools vs Skill

Learn new tools but be cautious about building your entire career on a tool. Focus on improving your skills beyond one particular tool as this is a major key to job security.

We talked about the necessity of learning new tools in a previous tip but I'd like to take this a step further by clarifying that as beneficial as it is to be able to use multiple tools, your true value lies in your skills and abilities.

Would you be able to bring value to an experience, design process, research etc if you're given a different tool? This is the question I'd like you to constantly ask yourself. Improve your cognitive abilities and your design skills in such a way that no matter how frequent tools come and go, your value will stay the same or increase.

Here's a secret, at the core of every tool within a particular descipline, majority of the functions are the same - especially in UX. With the exception of a few differences and upgrades, most tools do the same thing - maybe one better than the other. The only thing that you have to really learn is how to achieve these same functions using the different interfaces, flow, or process.

Be less intimidated by the different tools and focus on using them as tools that are there to help you make your work easier.

You are in control. You are the value.

Tip 45 - Ultimate Tool

Your favorite and ultimate tool should be your pen, pencil, marker, paper, or whiteboard. Being able to sketch your ideas down on a tangible medium traditionally is the most useful tool designers can boast of.

Technologies change and resources deplete, but the one thing that remains a constant across generations is print medium. It is a key part of your design process. Sketching and ideation are best done by hand because they give the designer the freedom and flexibility to get creative, make mistakes and truly convey their raw thoughts before any iterations. These sketches can also be digitized afterwards and refined if needed.

Though there is nothing wrong with being tech-centered during our process, it helps to be able to unplug and get our thoughts down with the least interruption possible.
You'll miss the millions of notifications etc. that do pull us from our train of thoughts every so often during the design process.

It is an experience on its own for those of you that aren't doing this yet. Try incorporating this into your process to see if it boosts your brainstorming and sketching sessions. I hope it does,

I always keep a pencil and a tiny notebook on hand. Ideas come at "random" times.

Tip 46 - Human-Centeredness

Be language conscious. Accessibility goes beyond being able to see. Use language that transcends color, race, societal classes etc. Designing for humans in today's world is more crucial than ever. Designers are now tasked with building products that fosters fruitful relationships among all groups of people. You are a design professional and now this responsibility is on your shoulders too.

Language is more than words. The types of words and combinations thereof, used in an experience can sway the emotion of the user from good to worse and vice versa. We design for emotion and this is pivotal to respecting the differences, similarities and humanity of our users.

Aside designing for audiences you are familiar with, there are times when you will be called to design for a new audience - one that is foreign to you. It is important that you approach this duty with the same level of delicacy, respect, empathy, and immersion into this new "world" of your users.

Becoming one with your users, understanding their behavior and building solutions that generate effective results will be your hidden power to succeeding in contributing to a better world through design.

Be human-centered.

Tip 47 - Size Hierarchy

Employ size hierarchy in your interfaces. Use sizing of elements to depict order of importance and direct customer action. Call-to-action buttons can be slightly larger than "regular" buttons, important sections can be wider than the others, header typography can be bigger than other texts, and so on. The trick here is to visually create a distinguisher between important elements in a tasteful but also easily recognizable way.

Similar to Content Hierarchy where information of high priority is displayed first to the user, you can also highlight relevant components using size differenctiation. Conversely, you can use this method to supress less relevant information as well.

Please be cautious to not over emphasize important information. This can be a deterring factor for task completion and conversion. Users do want to be informed and assisted throughout an experience but they also do not want to feel like they're being yelled at the entire time.

Everything can be useful in moderation,
but use this to your advantage.

Size matters.

Tip 48 - User Activity

Denote the past, present and the future. What has already happened, what is happening and what is about to happen. Creating an experience that solves user needs involves reducing the amount of guess-work required as much as possible. A major part of user experience is completing specific tasks, and this demands insight into the status of a user's actions.

At any given point in time, a user is either reading (receiving information), taking an action (clicking a trigger pint), entering information (typing or speaking), or waiting for a result (downloading, task completion etc.). A key method of keeping your user's attention is keeping them informed throughout the various states they may be in. It may seem minute but a very critical piece to a seamless customer journey.

This is also an opportunity to introduce moments of delight and retain customer attention as they interact with your experience.

Downloading, please wait...

Application received. Redirecting to the homepage...

Are you still here? System will reload in X seconds...

Our data monkeys will be with you shortly...

Have fun with this, it is a great way to be side-by-side with your user throughout a journey.

They want to be in the know, almost always.

Tip 49 - Mobile

Mobile design should always follow native platform best practices for optimal experience. Advocate for native versions unless hybrid tools account for and satisfy the majority of native rules.

Mobile technology is ever-improving, and though designing for mobile-web is a great shortcut to providing a mobile experience, designing native experiences reduces compatibility issues across platforms to create a more enjoyable and seamless experience.

For instance, Apple users are familiar with certain tricks and functions in their native applications, and so are Android users. We can try to build for a middle-ground but to truly capture your user's full attention and usability; you need to speak their language.

In-app animations, micro-interactions, terminology, language, flows etc, remain distinct across platforms. Unless your product resources cannot accommodate this, advocate for native development when you can. In cases where this is not possible, ensure that you follow posted design guidelines for each platform even as you build for a hybrid, mobile web.

Browser compatibility will also play a role in ensuring a smooth experience across the board.
Gather platform data from your users and design accordingly.

Tip 50 - Confirmation

Never forget about a confirmation step for detrimental or permanent actions. Humans make mistakes, and that is why this extra warning is highly important.

You don't have to overthink it; a simple "Are you sure you want to do "X"? will suffice. This tip is one of those no-brainers but easily forgotten features of the experiences we build. User research will always reveal areas of your experience that require a warning alert before a user can continue.

I've heard arguments about the "number of clicks" and "speed of task completion". The issue with prioritizing speed over caution is that the cost of a "speedy" accident by your user could mean losing an entire user group, valuable data, or ruined application reputation. Data is today's gold, and must be handled securely and cautiously. Allowing the user to double-opt in also relieves the company of any subsequent accusations of error on their part.

Sometimes our users do not fully understand the cost of an action, but they take it anyway. Our job is to protect them from making dire, irreversible mistakes in relation to sensitive and important data.

Lastly, you could also introduce a "version-control" system that a user can refer to later in case they changed their mind or want to revert a previous action.

Tip 51 - Consistency

Be sure to maintain consistency in your user journey and application experience. One very important distinguisher of a quality experience is the consistency of its visual elements, language, design, and overall experience. Think of it like a "brand style-guide". It makes for an enjoyable experience with very little surprises or frustration if you keep a consistent flow.

Even in the language you use, there is something to be said about consistency. If you use the word "Yes" as a confirmation trigger, keep that consistent throughout your application. An example of an inconsistent use of language is using "Yes" to confirm an action on one screen and then using "Okay" to confirm an action on another screen. The wording of your notification alerts, call-to-actions, etc., all add up to better comprehension and ease-of-use.

Keep your visual style consistent as well. This part is a lot easier to do in cases where there is already a design system and a brand style-guide but in other cases, you would have to do this subconsciously as you design. Either way, it is your duty to create consistency, cohesiveness, and harmony through the experiences you create.

Parts of the user journey may be different, but an overall consistent experience is still a requirement that nicely brings it all together.

I used the word consistency five times in this tip.

Tip 52 - Call-to-actions

Call-to-actions must be actionable. Use labels that persuade the user to act, and in the process, feel like they are taking an action. Often, we overlook the important a minor edit like this and fall back into the use of regular call-to-action (CTA) labels. Though they do work, a major part of increasing conversion is making your CTA's actionable.

It's a more personal experience and users somehow feel like they are the ones in control, which is what you want. Here are some examples:

"Show me my heat map,"

"Submit my order,"

"Request Delivery,"

"No, I do not want to receive promotional offers."

"Yes, I enjoyed my service,"

"Yes, I love my 101 Random UX Tips book."

Please keep in mind that CTA's transcend buttons. This tip applies to all CTA's, including any text, component, visual element, hyperlink, checkbox, multi-select, etc. in an interface that requires a user to take an action.

Keep it personal and actionable.

Tip 53 - Responsive Design Testing

Use real devices when testing responsive design. Building for responsiveness means designing and developing reactive elements that automatically update based on the user's behavior and platform environment. Lately, many digital applications allow designers to test for this digitally. So, instead of having to find every version of Apple iPhones, Android, and Google Phones, designers can test a wide range of devices directly on their desktop without having to use a real device. This is truly a super convenient and useful feature but I suggest testing on an actual device in moments where it is possible.

Technological developments are moving at the speed of light these days. To solely depend on digital tests getting updated as fast as operational system (OS) updates may be risky.

Use modern tools to your advantage of course, but when possible, do your testing on real devices because they will provide you with the most accurate feedback on your responsive interface performance.

Tip 54 - Micro-interactions

If and when you have the time, design for interaction. The tiny details and moments of surprise are the icing on your UX cake. Micro-interactions are a great way to keep your users engaged through an experience.

For instance, an animated and active progress bar keeps the user informed of the state of a download as they wait. The most popular use of micro-interaction is that seen in the animation on a "Like" button on Facebook and the double-tap to like button on Instagram. These short animations create excitement as well as a confirmation or status update after an action is performed.

Because keeping your users informed at all times is very important, you can use less server bandwidth by designing interfaces that incorporate tiny animated elements. Less full page reloads, popups, confirmation modals and extra clicks.

In actuality, micro-interactions can be animated GIFs, SVGs, or CSS Animation. Modern prototyping tools also have inbuilt drag-and-drop features for easy micro-interaction creation.

Allow your curiosity and creativity to flow into the details of your interaction design and watch your user experiences improve.

Refer to Page 60 for supporting tip.

Tip 55 - Lorem Ipsum

Go the extra mile and use real, sample content instead of "Lorem Ipsum" as placeholders. This is another practical way of setting your work apart. Though it certainly is easier to use Lorem Ipsum texts as placeholders, using sample content can be a great opportunity to add humor, and better convey content direction for the writing team during presentations.

You won't be penalized if you don't do this in your work. I understand that time constraints can limit your ability to do more but if you have the time, ensure that you add text content, illustrations or images that closely resemble your projected output. Text content is the more common way to achieve this.

In large teams, after your design is ready to be presented for feedback or even handed over to the dev team, your content team/writers will reach out to you to get more clarification on the type of content needed for your placeholders. Using sample content will save time and convey this message directly.

You may be required to do all the content writing if you're on a smaller team. This tip will also benefit you greatly when you come back in to write full content. Your sample text will serve as a guide for you to build on as you write.

You can begin with one sample sentence in areas with longer text content and continue the remaining with lorem ipsum text. It's really up to you to get creative.

Tip 56 - Opt-in

Respect your users' sovereignty in opting in to lists or triggering site features. Avoid automatically signing up your users for features that can be optional. Your users trust you with their data, and it is critical to understand the size of this responsibility.

Data selling is a revenue stream for some businesses and we're not here to judge, but an overarching principle can be applied to make such a business model beneficial for both the company and user involved. Users who find value in a product or service are willing to sign up for anything and everything recommended by the product. Focusing on producing a quality and valuable products can be an automatic magnet to getting all the opt-ins you're looking for.

On the other hand, if a company uses deceptive methods to sign users up for lists or features without transparent communication, consent, and awareness, this could lead to a catastrophe. Users have no fear of reporting to business bureaus, leaving terrible reviews and letting the world know its deceptive business practices.

Repairing a ruined company reputation costs more than building valuable products that attract willing users.

Let the user choose you for a reason.

Tip 57 - Reinvention

Don't reinvent the wheel but if you're going to reinvent, make sure it is an obviously better solution. We as designers sometimes get too excited that we overkill on the concepts and redesigns. Majority of the interface layouts have been the same for years because they do work. To redesign them would require introducing a much better option that supersedes what was already there. Other widely accepted and used experiences are only so because users are more familiar with it.

You have two options - and here is where the dilemma is. You could completely rebuild legacy layout treatments and experiences but you may face an uphill battle of user education and user adoption or you could take the road most traveled and save time, a lot of it. One could still be successful in reinventing the wheel but I believe it is important to understand what the scope of such an undertaking looks like before you begin.

Humans are habitual creatures and can be hesitant to change. Be sure to come ready to convince, ready to sway, and ready to impress. This could be your chance to make a name for yourself in the industry.

Do not be afraid, but do due diligence and execute.

Tip 58 - Conversion over Design

When you are in a dilemma of choosing between prioritizing design and conversion, choose conversion. It is harder to win-back lost customers than to update design elements, style or layout. Subsequently, when you go with conversion, make sure it is design-centered.

My wife disagrees very strongly with this tip. She is a Senior Graphic Designer with extensive experience and major clients; I respect her view on this, but as a UX designer, our main focus is based on ensuring that our users can perform their tasks successfully. This is why I prioritize conversion or usability success over aesthetic design. You could design a visually appealing interface, and though it may appear beautiful, it still misses usability success.

You're probably thinking, why not design a beautiful and effective interface at the same time? And that's a valid question but the reality is there comes a time when you get stuck at the crossroads of choosing between make a component beautiful or usable. That time will come, and when it does, prioritize usability before aesthetics. Afterward, come back in and upgrade the visual design.

Please note this tip does not disprove the importance of visual design but rather highlights its order of importance within the design process.

Tip 59 - Problem Statement

Define the problem from your users point-of-view. This is the best way to create solutions that work genuinely. Unless you're doing product design and prioritizing stakeholder-driven features, always dig deeper and truly step into the shoes of your user when defining the problem statement.

We throw around the word empathy a lot. Walking in the shoes of our users mean actually walking in their shoes and going where they go, immersing oneself into their world, from their point-of-view, and fully encountering their experience.

If your problem statement requires you to visit a location, do it. If it requires you to sit with your users or observe from a distance, do it. If it requires you to limit certain privileges you may currently have to grasp the experience of your user, do it.

Go the distance, immerse yourself in the world of your user and you will have a greater vantage point when defining your problem-statement.

It does require more effort than sitting behind a screen, but it serves as a priceless guide in your design direction and experience success.

Tip 60 - Call-to-action

Ensure that call-to-actions stand out - visually. Page content, elements, and texts that blend in with call-to-actions make it difficult for the user to identify how to proceed in an experience. There are many ways to create visual distinctions between interface components, and these include:

- Depth of Field
- Typography Styling (Bold, Italics, Underlined)
- Color Variations
- Size
- White/Negative Space
- Illustration and Imagery

Regardless of how you choose to implement this tip, setting call-to-actions apart in a manner that compliments your overall interface is what counts.

Refer to Page 64 for supporting tip.

Tip 61 - UX or UX

What matters the most in the user experience of an app?

...The Experience.

Are users having a successful and enjoyable experience when using the application or an unpleasant and frustrating one? A lot of UX designers automatically classify outdated interfaces or visually unappealing interface as "needing UX," but the truth is, as long as the users of that particular application are satisfied and "happy", the app has been "UXed".

Our goal as UX professionals is to meet the needs and satisfaction of our users. If the choice of our users look different than our own individual choice, we must honor the user choice over ours. It's all about what our users want - their happiness and satisfaction.

UX as a discipline is selfless, even amidst all our expertise and experience. Being able to let go of our own ideals and wishes to satisfy that of a user group is our top priority.

If your users are fully satisfied, then you did a great job.

Tip 62 - E-commerce

E-commerce is to the digital world what a storefront is to the physical world. It is a place where your customers encounter your service or product and you encounter them.
A great rule of thumb is to mimic your online experience to your in-store experience as close as possible and that will provide a better customer experience.

The most effective and high-converting e-commerce websites are ones that are able to bridge the gap between in-person (customer) experience and online (user) experience. Follow your customer's journey as you would in real-life to identify important checkpoints where there is a need to offer great customer service.

From the moment they first arrive to the time they leave or decide to, this is a potential customer and you would want to convert them before it's too late.

Do you have a door greeter, welcoming environment, attractive product display, brand authority, deals and promotions, seamless checkout, and customer appreciation measures in place?

When you start envisioning your online store as a physical location where you and your customers collide, you build an experience that works.

Tip 63 - Directions/Tool-tips

Assume less, explain more. Never assume that your user automatically knows what to do next - even in widely-used interface components. It is better to assume you need to direct the customer through every step of the journey than to risk their rage or frustration. Your system may require special input different from the norm and this is why it can be very helpful to provide directions and useful tips throughout your interface.

It's like offering a helping hand to someone. They can decide to accept it or decline and move on. Either way, the end result you're looking for is more likely to be achieved if the user can successfully progress through the experience.

You can include these guides and tips either via labels, subtitles, alternative texts, captions, modal popups, tool-tips or rollover messages. However, you decide to do it, make it useful.

User personas do not always represent 100 percent of your user demographics. Adding tool-tips and guides are a way to reach users that fall outside of your initial scope.

If our jobs are to make the life of the user easier, why not go the extra mile to make sure we achieve this goal? In order to build great experiences, your attitude should be like that of a live chat representative:

"Is there anything else I can help you with?".

Tip 64 - Learning Curve

If you're going to make your users learn something new, make it super easy to learn. The ease-of-use of your application experience can be a deterrent to some users and can also affect software adoption.

Human behavior can be difficult to change, though not impossible. Making your application experience easy, or second nature to use your application automatically widens your potential market-share even before you go to market.

The easiest commodity to sell, in my opinion, is convenience. As UX professionals, we build to make the life of the user easier and more convenient. This is our product - great experiences, useful features, convenient life.

Design with ease-of-use in mind. Do not let this limit you but rather guide your creativity as you build. Use conventional UI designs as stepping stones in building better and easy-to-use experiences.

Remember, the easier it is to use,
the higher your adoption rate.

Tip 65 - Display Architecture

Display information to your user in order of priority and importance. To account for the dwindling attention span of humans today, information must be delivered strategically. There are times when the info needed from the user is so critical that it is highly important to move it up the list and get that info upfront before requesting other relevant information.

For example, at one of the companies I contracted for, we moved the email field all the way up into a pop-up which was triggered after a user clicked "Add to cart". Displaying information in order of importance sometimes mean you have to move it to an entire different point in the user flow. We did this to be able to recover abandoned carts in case the user fails to checkout after adding a product to their cart. This widened our net for collecting email data and retargetting our missed customers with a promotional discount afterwards. We also moved the email field up to the first form field on the checkout page for this same purpose. (It was auto-populated).

This is somewhat similar to Information Architecture but still different. It is not necessarily how you arrange information to be found by your users but how you display that info at any given point.

You, the company and user data gets to decide which piece of information is more important than the other. This translates to how you will display this info in order to collect the right data in the right order before you lose the attention of your customer.

Tip 66 - System Status

Inform users of your system status at all times. In a world where technology is rising at the speed of light, we can assume that users are doing their best to keep up. We can't assume that users know what is happening behind the scenes when they trigger an action.

The best way to keep our users at peace throughout experiences is to inform where possible, the current system/server status behind the scene.

Companies are even going to the extent of developing focused system pages that are updated in real-time on system functionality and status. Those systems are on a larger scale but we can transmit this same concept into call-to-actions on a feature experience.

If the system is retrieving a file for download, please say so.

If the system is processing my payment method, please say so.

If the system is sending me an email shortly, please let the user know.

You can also take this a step further into service operations and ensure that the user is informed of the system (order, service, ticket, request, etc) status at frequent intervals. You reduce user frustration and create a pleasant experience through the transparency of information.

Tip 67 - Mobile

Ensure that mobile call-to-action elements are large enough for users to tap easily. Take into consideration average thumb/finger sizes and mobile habits.

When designing for mobile, be practical. Thumb and finger sizes are not the same with all users. Think through the flow of your experience and assess whether it compliments current mobile interaction habits or creates more work for the user.

The majority of mobile users primarily use their thumbs for mobile control. Fore-fingers are mostly used for secondary controls. Take these into consideration for spacing between elements, size of elements, on-screen positioning, sticky or non-sticky, floating elements, information, and display hierarchy. You would want to center your mobile experience around ease-of-use all the way through.

Can your user progress through a journey easily with limited error clicks (taps)?

If you can reduce the number of error taps in your mobile user experience, you're one step away from building an effective mobile interface.

Tip 68 - Sticky Magic

Use sticky elements to your advantage.
Sticky technology allows interface elements to stay within view even as users scroll or navigate away from their current viewport. This is a great way to keep important components in front of your users at all times.

Be sure to consider this technology for the interfaces you build. Which parts of your experience could benefit from being fixed on screen while the user continues through other parts of the customer journey. The most widely used sticky elements are Shopping Carts, Navigation Menus, Forms, and Call-to-actions. You will see these in conversion-heavy experiences.

Nonetheless, sticky is not limited to these use-cases. Feel free to take it a step further and include it in your experiences.

User feedback and data will prove useful or otherwise.

Tip 69 - Breadcrumbs

Include breadcrumbs in your experiences. Humans hate to be lost, unless they willingly embarked on an adventure. Breadcrumbs serve as a digital compass for users. Informing a user of their current location in your experience is a great way to keep them engaged and at peace knowing how far they have gone, and how much more there is to go to complete a task.

Users assume a lot during unsure moments. Leaving your user to guess the estimated time or steps left can be a scary bet to take. They may either assume more steps remain or none left only to be surprised and end up frustrated at whatever the next step holds.

In other scenarios, users like the option to return to a previous step in an experience. Browser "back" buttons sometimes fail to serve this purpose if the site mapping is not laid out according to the journey. This is a dev issue. But nonetheless, your user would still like the option to go back as they wish. Breadcrumbs make it easy for them to do so without losing site of the full user journey in a specific task.

> Breadcrumbs are like real estate,
> it's all about the location.

Tip 70 - Contract or Full-time

This tip is as much a UX tip as it is a Career Tip. I receive this question a lot of which one is better: a contract gig or a full-time role. The answer is simple: it depends on the candidate's needs and goals.

If you're looking for something with more guarantee then a full-time role may be the better option. Even then, I would also argue that a contract role could be a better option since most of them could be 12 or 24-month contracts. In a scenario like that you are sure to be employed for that amount of time. In contrast, a full time role could last shorter based on volatile factors such as changing business needs etc. This applies to contract as well but at least you have a promise of an employment time frame.

The other point is that a full time job usually comes with health insurance benefits and if that is something you're looking for, then that's a better option.

Lastly, contract roles may be a better option if you're looking to add big brand names to your resume. Large companies tend to hire for more contract work than others. You could snatch a few to get a decorated resume and experience. Full time roles with large companies are harder to get.

The list goes on and on but I hope the pros and cons above give you a good place to start as you decide on your next steps.

Tip 71 - Hover on Mobile

Replace hover effects on mobile with something more user friendly. As you are aware, mobile interfaces generally do not use mouse or cursor interactivity. It's mostly a tap, pull, drag or swipe.

Certain experiences account for hover effects through a press and hold feature. The issue with that is the user may be unaware if they're not notified of this functionality. It can also be a bit frustrating since the "hold time" differs from one experience to another. Mobile hover technology is still a work in progress in my opinion.

Hover effects on desktop are amazing, and can be left alone. When these effects translate to mobile, that's where we could replace the hover with an "auto-load", a tool-tip, tap-to-reveal etc. Build an alternative to your desktop hover in your mobile experience, and this will bridge the gap between desktop and mobile for the benefit of both you and the user.

It doesn't really matter which platform you design for first, always ensure that they complement each other in their features.

Tip 72 - Mobile Modal

Use mobile modals wisely - ensure that the exit button is noticeable, properly-sized, and placement is optimal.

Modal popups were meant to be used for actionable confirmation content when it was first introduced but have quickly become a window for any and all things.

Popup usage can be abused. Keep modal features reserved for actionable and relevant information. The mass adoption by designers has revealed certain flaws in modal usage on mobile. The truth is modals are everywhere now but they perform poorly on mobile phones and tablets.

Exit buttons and texts are either too small to tap, poorly placed, or hidden completely as a way to force the user through a specific channel. Consider mobile usage data and how your users interact with your application on mobile. If you have more single-handed users then consider navigation placement on the bottom-fold of the screen. If you have double-handed users, both top and bottom could suffice. Also think through full-screen modals, overlays, sticky modals etc.

Take the time to explore all the different modal factors and pull in characteristics that would serve your users well on mobile.

Tip 73 - User Attention

Give every user what they want when it comes to information. Some users want all the details, others want only the key points, the rest want a blend of both.

Research has found that users come in groups and these groups take certain actions based on how much information they have or do not have. During online shopping for instance, certain users will shop on the catalog page by simple adding multiple products to their cart. Others will click into each product to get more details before adding to cart. An in-between user group will use the "Quick View" feature to view a summary description of the product within the same catalog page (sometimes a pop-up or drop-down with product summary). In my opinion, you have to provide all three options tastefully if you're going to win.

Find a way to give each of the three main user groups what they want - full details, detail summary, or only key specifications.

Sometimes we focus too much on either simplifying or improving information that we forget about other user groups.

Tip 74 - Interaction Time

Micro interactions are amazing additions to interface design but the amount of time the animation take should be no more than two seconds for optimal experience.

Sometimes, designers forget to take note of the animation times as they dig deeper into building amazing micro-interactions. User attention is dwindling as we know it, and an opportunity to add a moment of delight can quickly turn into user frustration and a lost customer if it's dragged out.

Keep your micro-interactions short and straight to the point. Just a sprinkle of joy where needed. The other aspect of sprinkling joy is to do this at strategic checkpoints in your experience. Refrain from adding too many micro-interactions unless of course you are designing for the younger generation who live off animations.

Make it awesome but don't make it gimmicky.

Tip 75 - Documentation

Develop a habit of documentation. Keeping records of completed prototypes, work in progress, project scopes, ideas, concepts, design review feedback and even team meeting minutes can come in handy later on in so many ways.

I can't tell you enough how an idea that was later accepted to be developed by stakeholders had already been proposed by me months prior. Documenting such thoughts and ideas make it easier to have something to show to prove your workmanship and dedication. This is not the only use-case but for project scope, it could be very helpful again later on if team members or stakeholders decide to adjust the ask without prior notice.

Writing and documentation in general is a very necessary characteristic any designer should have. They are like receipts for anything you purchase. You never know when you may need to return an item or even prove that you did purchase it.

Build the habit of taking notes, recording your thoughts, processes and storing ideas in a safe place. As a human, you yourself may even need to come back to it later on.

Tip 76 - Execution

Execution is everything. The UX discipline has so many points of execution and this gives designers several opportunities to sweep clients and stakeholders off their feet. It's like a well prepared meal with no garnish. You couldn't really tell if the look will compliment the taste or otherwise. On the other hand, a beautifully garnished meal's taste is expected to compliment the look.

During your research process, you have the opportunity to document your research data in an easy to understand presentation or document that can be shared with stakeholders and team members. One that fully breaks down research data into comprehensible chunks.

During your design process, you have an opportunity to assemble your work in the most beautiful slides, PDFs or presentations to be viewed and shared. The animation, summary, detail and content copy are all garnish that makes your work stand out.

Final prototypes need all the love in the world to draw desired emotion from users and stakeholders. Pull in complimentary elements to include in your work to set it apart. Practice your speech. Prepare your outfit, everything counts. You are in charge here.

The main factor to understand is that your execution will be everything, so do it well.

Tip 77 - Dev Teams

Build a relationship with your development team. They are the ones who ultimately bring our design prototypes to life. Even though many designers have a love-hate relationship with their development team, I challenge you to purposefully (and strategically) build a relationship with them. The front end development team especially.

The benefits of doing this is enormous. In summary, they will be on your side and be more willing to take a stab at that crazy idea of yours if there's a relationship there. You would have to be intentional and it will require effort from you.

Setup a lunch date with your developers. Genuinely get to know them. They are human as you are and have individual likes, hobbies, family, fears, strengths and weaknesses. You will be surprised how many similarities you may have in common with others on your team.

After all, you are a human-behavioral designer so immerse yourself into your humanity and that of others. Set a great example with your best foot forward and watch the benefits stack up.

Additionally, if you can, bring them coffee every now and then. I don't know, but just ideas. The point is to build a genuine relationship with them. You're all on the same team and team building is critical to team success.

Be the champion.

Tip 78 - Work Attachment

Do not be too attached to your work. Your emotional connection can interfere with your sound judgment and prioritization of user needs over yours.

We love our work, that's what makes us designers. As a matter of fact, every human loves the things they create. In our world though, since we create for the satisfaction of others, there is an invisible line that separate designing for self satisfaction and designing for user satisfaction. A good designer is able to let go of his own ideas and concepts for one that may better serve the users.

Continue to love the work you create, it will be almost impossible to ask you not to. But while you love, recognize that you have a duty to perform and that duty is one that satisfies your user.

Be attached to user satisfaction instead of your work. You do work to satisfy the user not vice versa.

Tip 79 - Listen Actively

Listen to understand, not to respond. Do more listening than talking. Talk less, listen more. This is a rule of thumb that applies to several aspects of your design career.

Listening actively to
- stakeholder requests,
- your users,
- team feedback,
- during user research etc.

The list goes on and on. Being patient enough to absorb information, comprehend it fully and then provide feedback is one form of discipline that builds character and skill.

Aside the fact that you retain majority of the information being received, you also subtly convey the importance of the speaker through your attentiveness.

Refrain from finishing people's sentences, and composing a response while they're actively speaking. Allow them to complete their thoughts, before you proceed to formulate a response.

Tip 80 - Portfolio

Find a way to add personality to your portfolio. UX portfolios have become a formality these days so much so that we have lost the touch of our very discipline: the human touch. Portfolios mostly consist of projects and everything else but the human (designer) behind it.

You have a story, a background, hobbies, extra skills, quirks etc that make you unique. Your portfolio is space that allows you the creative freedom to express your humanity in addition with your professional accolades. Do not limit yourself to only professional experience. You may actually be missing out on shared hobbies or interests with teams and hiring managers who would love to just chat and see how it goes.

I've seen some designers include gifs of themselves at a dance class, or kayaking to add a human touch to their portfolio. Others have a video of themselves speaking about their achievements, goals and passions. I've also seen animated calligraphy hero images that represented a designer who's hobby was calligraphies and hand lettering.

If you like The Office, throw some favorite lines or memes in there. Just an example but the possibilities are endless. Be yourself, be human.

Tip 81 - Mental Health

You are not a robot, take care of your mental health. It is almost a guarantee that life's up and downs will take a toll on you as time goes by. Being aware of the need to maintain your physical and mental health is key to a successful career and life in general.

Start with your physical health. Maintain an active lifestyle by exercising regularly. As designers, we mostly spend hours sitting behind our computers and losing track of time. Getting up to walk about after every hour or two is a great way to keep your muscles stretched and your eyes rested after staring at a screen for that long. While you stay active, watch your food intake and eat well. Eat healthy foods that provide you with nourishing nutrients to keep your body able and functional. You can't really do your job if you're not well. Lastly, drink responsibly - it matters.

When things get difficult, do not be afraid to talk about your feelings. Talking about your feelings and confronting issues head-on can help you deal with them as they come. Ask for help when needed. We all need assistance in various aspects from time to time. Walk away and take a break if you need to. You deserve to give your body and brain a break to rejuvenate.

Do things that bring you peace and keep you in the best spirits. Life can get hard, you are all your body's got.

Tip 82 - Job Search

Build professional experience by doing professional work. It doesn't always have to be paid, your professional experience is worth more in the long run than any payment you will receive.

Majority of today's job descriptions require a minimum of one to two years of experience. This can be hard to achieve for new graduates. The way you stock up on professional experience is by pursuing work for startups, charities, small businesses and even volunteer work. It's difficult to get a job without experience and I understand that bills have to be paid at the same time but sometimes if it means taking a regular job in order to maintain a good standard of living while you work on your professional portfolio, that may be a better option.

Your bootcamp experience cannot qualify as professional experience. Paid or unpaid work for charities, startups etc would though. You get to really experience what it means to have real expectations from clients and deadlines to meet. Even unpaid clients are still very aggressive in their pursuit for work that is done well as it affects their revenue and bottom line.

My point is this, if you are in need of experience, be open to doing work that will get you the right level of experience to propel you for the ideal role you're looking for whether paid or unpaid. In the end, you will get paid well - very well.

Tip 83 - Leaving a company

Do not burn bridges, you may need them later. Leaving a company whether willfully or unwillingly can be a daunting experience but doing so in a way that ruins your relationship with the company, managers, team members, and hiring team can come back to bite you in future.
There is not a one-size-fits-all and people do not work at the same company forever so be sure to address any complaints in a way that's human, tasteful and respectable.

The reality is this, there will always be something or someone that does not mesh well with you. Yet, you are responsible for your actions and reactions. Your professionalism will be a soft skill that proves useful at that same company or another. You grow when you build a certain level of tolerance and self control.

There are legal ways to resolve employment issues. Taking an appropriate approach to resolving employment conflicts is a good trait to have as a designer.

The bridges you keep will evolve into a powerful professional network to count on in future.

Tip 84 - Devices

Use modern and newer devices in your portfolio mock-ups. This is one of the tricks from a designers toolbox that sets their portfolio apart. Most designers overlook this and are unaware of how much a small change such as this could affect the aesthetics of their work.

For example, a portfolio with mobile mock-ups of iPhone 5 will appear old-fashioned merely because there are several newer models that have been released in recent years. The fact that most free mock-up resources online may not be updated quickly enough doesn't mean designers can't take a photo of newer devices themselves for mocking up prototypes. Sometimes you have to get your hands dirty and take your own photographs or compositions as needed.

Lastly, keeping your mock-up devices and compositions up-to-date also conveys a message of technological awareness to the hiring manager in a unique way.

You benefit from good aesthetics and being in the know.

Tip 85 - Your Role

Clearly state your role and contribution to a project in your portfolio. Most designers assume the summary or project description is enough to inform hiring managers of their role on an assignment.
I've seen portfolios that highlight impressive interface designs but fail to specify the designers role. Upon my prodding, I find out that the designer didn't really work on the entire piece or vice versa.

Sometimes an entire interface experience is misinterpreted by the hiring manager to be designed by a team if not clearly specified by the designer. "UX" the hiring manager as well. Approach them as if they were a user because they are. And if everything is conveyed accurately on your portfolio you may enjoy the benefits desired.

Clarity will breed comprehension.

Tip 86 - Tools

Tools are important. Your proficiency in various design tools can be a factor in your candidacy for a role. Though not the only factor, sometimes companies hire for specific needs and may not have the bandwidth to train new employees on new tools.

Be sure to clearly state the types of tools you used on a particular project. Even better, add a brief on how these tools were used and your level of proficiency in each one. If there are more tools you are learning, you should also include that and any goals you have set for those.

Please understand that tools are not your saving grace but they can be a helper in identifying roles or teams that will be a better fit for you at any stage in your career.

Tip 87 - Community

Join a design community - a digital one and a physical one. People always say humans weren't meant to be alone, and there is some truth to that because aside the obvious benefits of having community, there are mental benefits that come with it as well.

Physical communities promote good social skills and digital communities widen our circle of friends and associates.

As a designer, a community will play an integral role in your skill-set development. Whether it be a design-centered meetup group, a book club, social media connections, or national organizations, you get to interact and build priceless relationships with different people across your city and country. These relationships can span a lifetime and bear fruits in many ways such as career recommendations, workshops, speaking engagements, book gigs etc.

Plug in, it's beneficial to be a part of something other than oneself.

Tip 88 - User Audio

Collect audio during user testing if you can. Your ability to listen to the reactions of users while they interact with your experience is another key to obtaining authentic feedback.

Users (humans) react audibly during moments of uncertainty, frustration and excitement. These are good clues in identifying the emotion of the user at given checkpoints in an experience.

Advocate for video with audio capability but if the technology is not available, make the best of your research and extract quality feedback through other research methods.

Building amazing products means deriving quality feedback to influence design direction whether with audio capabilities or otherwise.

Tip 89 - UX World

Obtain general knowledge about other types of UX roles outside of Application Experience Design because it is always good to broaden your knowledge base, learn new trends, and secure a future in the industry if tides change.

I've been super curious about Voice User Experience Design (VUI) lately. It's an entirely different world of UX that shares a lot of similarities but involves slightly different approaches. Super cool to listen in on related talks and how VUI designers work. Other roles I've heard of are Learning Designers who mostly focus on crafting learning platforms, Instructional Designers who do something similar, UX strategists who only focus on the strategy and direction of application experience, UX Product Manager who owns the design to development process and managing cross-functional product team to achieve product goals, UX Writers who solely focus on interface copy, language, and conversion-focused content.

There are so many UX-related roles that you may be unaware of. Feel free to explore the other areas and you might just find your next adventure!

Tip 90 - Self Assessment

Assess yourself honestly, identify gaps in your skills and work on improving them. We all have strengths and weaknesses, only a fool would assume that they have none. Do a self assessment and explore areas of your design process where you are strong and parts where you may need improving.

From the ideation and concepting phase, through the research phase - the gathering of user feedback and synthesis, wire-framing, lo-fi and hi-fi prototyping, design reviews, user testing, Q & A, etc there may be a step in the process that doesn't excite you and this aspect is where you should spend extra time to work on growing your skill set on that arena.

It pays to be a generalist. It does pay equally or better to be a specialist too but UX generalist jobs are more available than others. This makes it a more sought-after role which would mean your continuous growth in the entire product design process can be added value for employment.

Don't stop growing.

Tip 91 - Job Search

Be encouraged, your hard work will pay off. All the "sweat equity" you are investing into your career will bear fruit in due time. If it's any consolation, we have all been there. Hundreds and thousands of rejection letters, no responses and not-a-good-fits later, you get to a place where you won't have to apply for jobs anymore. Instead, the jobs come to you and sometimes (most times) you get to name your price.

The journey to this level requires effort and I will be doing you a huge disservice if I said it was easy. You will have to put in the work, the right way in order to get similar results. Human-Computer Interaction doesn't seem like it's going anywhere especially with the growing adaptation of modern technology. It is safe to say you are in great company and a great industry.

In due time, the floodgates will be open to shed some light on you and everything you bring to the table.

Though we've all been there, it can certainly be a frustrating experience going through the process. Do not be afraid to do the work, it pays.

Tip 92 - Portfolio Goals

Another tip for creating an effective portfolio is to add a "goals or next steps" section. This is an area where you let the hiring manager know about your career goals and next steps in the industry.

Why is this useful?
It is important to have a goal. And part of knowing where you are going sends a positive message to hiring managers about the type of individual they'll be working with. Many a times, we add the word "goal-oriented" to our resumes but they're only words until proven. Being vocal about your next career goals sends the right message and also aligns you with the right roles and companies.

This is also a great way to tell the hiring manager how interested you are in a particular role or industry.

If you truly have a set goal, then your job applications will be targeted, which will mean the right hiring managers will be viewing your portfolio and receiving the message of your interest in their industry, type of role or team.

Where do you see yourself going next in your career? Now, you have to think and plan.

Tip 93 - Why UX?

If you chose this career path solely because of the money and "getting rich quick", you are more likely to fail. The User Experience profession is a human-centered emotional role that requires passion. The entire process, design and development, testing etc. demand your full emotional availability and empathy. You must love your craft, if you're going to be successful. This is the only way to endure the ups and downs that the industry brings.

The discipline of UX does pay well. I heard someone say somewhere that UX professionals are now the lawyers of the tech world and that is very true. You have potential to earn anywhere from mid five-figures to six-figures. This doesn't come without its fair share of troubles though and that is why you must be passionate enough to withstand the trouble.

Why did you chose UX? Are you passionate enough about helping people and building incredible experiences that contribute to the effectiveness of human-computer interaction? Or are you just in it because you needed to switch jobs and find something that pays better.

UX can be draining and demanding because it is emotionally centered, are you passionate enough?

Tip 94 - Metrics

This tip is to bring to your attention the importance of knowing your UX metrics. There are key metrics or Key Performance Indicators (KPI's) that communicate the success or failure of a feature or experience. We will not dive deep into this but I wanted to highlight the importance of knowing these numbers.
Know which ones to track and how frequent to track them.

An easy way to determine which metrics to track is to go back to the problem statement and work your way forward. What is the initial user problem you are trying to solve for and how can you track the success of your solution? Would a simple Conversion Rate metric work or you may need a segmented, complex way to track your product success.

Sometimes you may need to keep an eye on two or three metrics in order to derive your desired metric.

Know your numbers and how your experience is doing. This will help you in refining your product to better serve your users.

Tip 95 - Interactive Prototypes

This tip affects two aspects of your design process. The first one is to be sure to include interactive prototypes or video interaction of your experiences in your portfolio. Secondly, be sure to use interactive prototypes during design presentations. This makes it easy to convey your user journey to stakeholders for better comprehension and buy-in.

Interactive prototypes add a nice touch to portfolios. They make it easy for hiring managers to experience your work in a functional state. This can also be a great opportunity to show or include micro-interactions for added points.

Putting interactive prototypes together are much easier today than they were 10 years ago. There are many tools that allow you to easily import your interface screens or even link pages directly within your design files to be exported as interactive or video files (.mov, .mpeg etc).

Look into the various tools and find one that you'd be able to use.

Tip 96 - Productivity

Find ways to maximize your productivity and time so that you can avoid burnout. Being a high output and high-performing designer requires a lot and sometimes rest, pace, strategy and process escapes our planning. For instance, there are times during the day when you are most productive, identify these times and prioritize major tasks to be completed within this window. High-priority tasks can be completed this during time and low priority tasks can be reserved for the times when you are performing at an average level. Personally, I take a nap during my low-performance window. This allows me to stay rested and rejuvenated throughout the day to pick back up when the window of opportunity arises again.

Early mornings are my high performing times, as well as late nights. In-between these times, I complete low-priority tasks that require less brain-power. This way I'm still getting things completed without wasting too much time doing nothing.

Lastly, procrastinate less. If you have a pending task, start it within the first 5 minutes if it being on your mind otherwise a distraction will set in and sweep away your thoughts. This is another way to stay alert and on top of things. And also, your calendar should be your friend.

Organization is key.

Tip 97 - Interviews

I have been in countless amounts of interviews at different levels in my career and one key tip I can offer about interviews is be ready to sell yourself.
An interview or introductory call is a meeting setup to measure whether you are a good fit for a role or otherwise. You are also interviewing the company and checking to confirm if you'll enjoy working at this company.

Come prepared. Prepare your speech and flow. Practice your interview several times over. This can be compared going to an audition, it is a big deal. Practice in your bathroom mirror or with family, do a mock interview where you are asked similar questions but also prepare you own selling points as to why you should be hired.

Being nervous is normal. Focus your energy on selling you, your value and expertise. When explaining your experience, be sure to dig a little deeper touching on key areas of a past role that adds value to the particular role you are interviewing for. Begin in descending order, starting with the major roles you held and then ending with the less major ones. Focus on emphasizing why you are the perfect match the role. This is how you sell yourself and confidently approach an interview process.

Tip 98 - Interviewing

Ask questions. Early on in my career, I held companies to so high of an esteem that I was uncomfortable asking any questions during an interview. That was a weak approach. Feel free to ask the interviewer questions.

Ask about the company and team culture. Ask about the team you will be working with and workflow. Ask questions about the industry and what sets that company apart from the rest. A really good question that I like is to ask the interviewer what made them join the company? This question also serves as an "icebreaker " even in the middle of the conversation. They then proceed to share their passion and authentic reasons for taking the role in the first place and what their experience has been with the company thus far. This gives you good insight into the company and even sparks great follow-up questions to keep the conversation going.

> The interviewer is human too,
> you can connect on a human level and be at peace during interviews.

Tip 99 - Company Sizes

Everyone wants to work at the large, major corporations of the world and this is why it is difficult to make it. There can only be so many positions and the other reality is that their interview process is vigorous and highly intimidating. Do not be discouraged if you are turned down several times over in your quest to work at a large firm. The time may just not be right yet and you may need more experience to be able to succeed through the process.

Sometimes smaller companies may have a more rewarding role, better aligned to suit your career goals, and even better benefits as well. The "name brand" of a company is great but being fulfilled in your role is more rewarding in the long run.

Companies come and go, but you, your sanity, your satisfaction, and your purpose stays.

Tip 100 - Content Creation

This is something I tell my mentees all the time. Start creating content. I used to hate reading and writing but when I came to the realization that helping others meant helping myself and developing better habits, I embraced content creation.

Creating content requires special commitment and discipline. It forces you to learn new tools, record your thoughts, plan content structure, delivery and so on.

Not only will you be producing content on a topic that you are passionate about and one that eventually adds value to your expertise; you grow as an individual and subject-matter expert.

The rewards are immense when you create useful content that benefits many. It can be an extension of your role and passion in helping others.

Tip 101 - Multiple Stakeholders

In scenarios where stakeholder asks are conflicting, set up an alignment meeting that addresses each stakeholders goals and defines a common core goal that all the stakeholders share.

Even though their individual agendas may conflict, there is going to be a common underlying goal that they can all agree on as a must-have to ensure product or company success. This is how you derive a broader goal and then strategically create features that address the individual goals of your stakeholders. Meet the common broader goals first and then explore ways of including secondary goals within your experience.

Setting up the alignment meeting is very important. Explain the need to identify a common goal across the stakeholders and how that will help drive design direction and product development. If an in-person meeting can't happen, try a digital one. If that's impossible as well, setup a shared document. It's all about finding a way to bring all their asks and thoughts together in one place to sort out and organize.

You can do this.

Tip 102 - Strategically Over-deliver

Always under-promise and over-deliver. Humans love elements of surprise, especially when they feel they are getting more. This tip is a bonus tip to prove this point. Start at your workplace and the tasks you are responsible for. Give yourself ample time to complete it to the best of your ability but if you are able, always try to go above and beyond - go that extra mile. It could be an extra feature that was planned for the next sprint, or some basic research that was needed, etc. Assess your workload and find ways by which you could go an extra mile. It doesn't have to be major additions every time, any icing on the cake will be a huge surprise to your team. It speaks very well of your workmanship and dedication to your craft.

There are times where you can
- complete your tasks before the deadline,
- put a great presentation together before the meeting,
- reach out to cross departmental team members to move a project along without waiting around,
- create an extra use-case for an experience as you design,
- fill in to assist a co-worker in order to move a project along, or
- burn the midnight candle in order to meet a deadline.

These are only ideas but they go a very long way being an employee willing to go the extra mile. Approach this from a place of delight. Delight in the opportunity you have to use your skills in incredible ways.